DISCARD

jBIO   Porter, Esther
WILLIAMS
            Serena Williams

07-07-16
            CHILDREN: BIOGRAPHY

Pebble® Plus

Women in Sports

SERENA WILLIAMS

by Esther Porter

CAPSTONE PRESS
a capstone imprint

Pebble Plus is published by Capstone Press,
1710 Roe Crest Drive, North Mankato, Minnesota 56003
www.mycapstone.com

Library of Congress Cataloging-in-Publication Data
Cataloging-in-Publication Data is on file with the Library of Congress.
ISBN 978-1-4914-7973-5 (library binding)
ISBN 978-1-4914-8569-9 (paperback)
ISBN 978-1-4914-8575-0 (eBook PDF)

Editorial Credits
Abby Colich, editor; Sarah Bennett, designer;
Eric Gohl, media researcher; Katy LaVigne, production specialist

Photo Credits
Getty Images: AFP/Philippe Huguen, 17, Ken Levine, 9; Newscom:
Atticusimages/Paul Harris, 7, Reuters/David Gray, 13, Reuters/Kevin
Lamarqu, 11, REX/Tony Kyriacou, 15, ZUMA Press/Brian Peterson,
19; Shutterstock: 1stGallery, back cover, 2, 24, Leonard Zhukovsky, 21,
Lev Radin, cover (background), 1, pdrocha, cover, 5, Suksamran1985, 9
(background), 15 (background), 17 (background), 21 (background), 22,
www.BillionPhotos.com, 3, 23

Note to Parents and Teachers

The Women in Sports set supports national curriculum standards for social
studies related to people, places, and culture. This book describes and
illustrates Serena Williams. The images support early readers in understanding
the text. The repetition of words and phrases helps early readers learn new
words. This book also introduces early readers to subject-specific vocabulary
words, which are defined in the Glossary section. Early readers may need
assistance to read some words and to use the Table of Contents, Glossary, Read
More, Internet Sites, Critical Thinking Using the Common Core, and Index
sections of the book.

Printed in the United States of America in North Mankato, Minnesota.
092015 009221CGS16

Table of Contents

A Tennis Family

Serena Williams was born September 26, 1981. She was the youngest of five girls. Her father, Richard, knew Serena would be a tennis champ.

Richard started teaching Serena
tennis when she was 3. She and
her sister Venus practiced every day.
Serena played in her first tournament
at age 4. By 1991 her record
was 46–3 in the USTA junior tour.

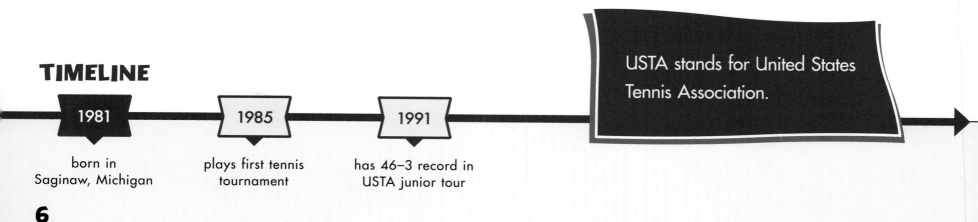

TIMELINE

1981

born in
Saginaw, Michigan

1985

plays first tennis
tournament

1991

has 46–3 record in
USTA junior tour

USTA stands for United States
Tennis Association.

Richard with Venus and Serena in 1991

By age 10 Serena was ranked first in her division. In 1991 Richard took her out of the junior tour. The family moved to Florida. Serena trained with a new coach.

TIMELINE

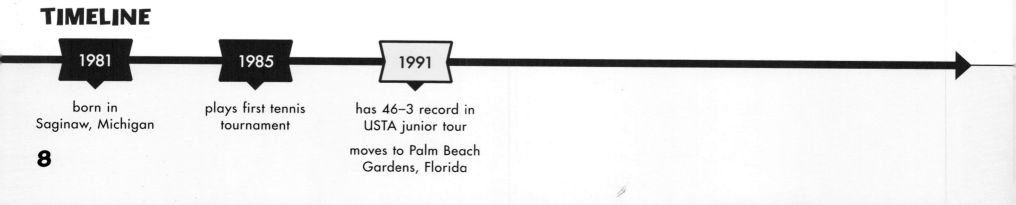

1981 — born in Saginaw, Michigan

1985 — plays first tennis tournament

1991 — has 46–3 record in USTA junior tour
moves to Palm Beach Gardens, Florida

Going Pro

Serena played in her first

pro tournament in 1995.

She lost in the first round.

Serena took time to improve.

In 1999 she won the U.S. Open.

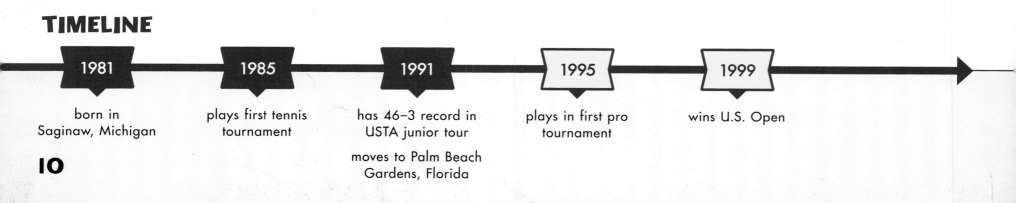

TIMELINE

1981	1985	1991	1995	1999
born in Saginaw, Michigan	plays first tennis tournament	has 46–3 record in USTA junior tour / moves to Palm Beach Gardens, Florida	plays in first pro tournament	wins U.S. Open

In July 2002 Serena was ranked first in the world. In 2002 and 2003, she won four straight Grand Slam titles. The media called this the "Serena Slam."

TIMELINE

1981	1985	1991	1995	1999	2002–2003
born in Saginaw, Michigan	plays first tennis tournament	has 46–3 record in USTA junior tour	plays in first pro tournament	wins U.S. Open	earns "Serena Slam"
		moves to Palm Beach Gardens, Florida			

SERENA SLAM

Serena Williams

13

Return from Injury

Serena beat Venus in the 2003 Wimbledon final. Then Serena injured her knee. For years she struggled to play. In 2007 she came back to win the Australian Open.

TIMELINE

1981	1985	1991	1995	1999	2002–2003
born in Saginaw, Michigan	plays first tennis tournament	has 46–3 record in USTA junior tour moves to Palm Beach Gardens, Florida	plays in first pro tournament	wins U.S. Open	earns first "Serena Slam"

2003

beats Venus
in the
Wimbledon final

2007

wins Australian
Open

15

Serena won the 2008 U.S. Open.

Then she and Venus won

Olympic gold in women's doubles.

By 2009 Serena's rank improved.

She won the Australian Open

and Wimbledon.

TIMELINE

1981	1985	1991	1995	1999	2002–2003
born in Saginaw, Michigan	plays first tennis tournament	has 46–3 record in USTA junior tour	plays in first pro tournament	wins U.S. Open	earns first "Serena Slam"
		moves to Palm Beach Gardens, Florida			

2003
beats Venus
in the
Wimbledon final

2007
wins Australian
Open

2008
wins U.S. Open
and Olympic
gold

2009
wins Australian
Open and
Wimbledon

The Champion Is Back

Serena injured her foot in 2010.

She came back to win

the 2012 Olympic gold medal

in women's singles. Serena and Venus

won gold again in women's doubles.

TIMELINE

1981	1985	1991	1995	1999	2002–2003
born in Saginaw, Michigan	plays first tennis tournament	has 46–3 record in USTA junior tour moves to Palm Beach Gardens, Florida	plays in first pro tournament	wins U.S. Open	earns first "Serena Slam"

2003
beats Venus
in the
Wimbledon final

2007
wins Australian
Open

2008
wins U.S. Open
and Olympic
gold

2009
wins Australian
Open and
Wimbledon

2012
wins Olympic
gold in singles
and doubles

Serena again won Wimbledon in 2015. It was her 21st Grand Slam win. She is the oldest female to be ranked number one. Some call her the best tennis player ever.

TIMELINE

1981	1985	1991	1995	1999	2002–2003
born in Saginaw, Michigan	plays first tennis tournament	has 46–3 record in USTA junior tour / moves to Palm Beach Gardens, Florida	plays in first pro tournament	wins U.S. Open	earns first "Serena Slam"

2003	2007	2008	2009	2012	2015
beats Venus in the Wimbledon final	wins Australian Open	wins U.S. Open and Olympic gold	wins Australian Open and Wimbledon	wins Olympic gold in singles and doubles	wins 21st Grand Slam title

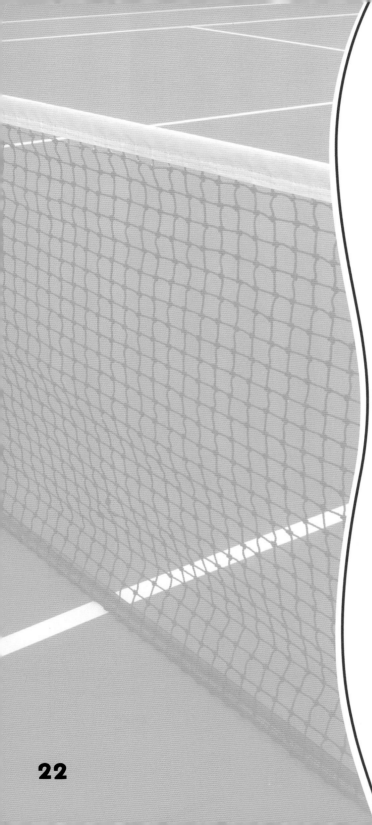

Glossary

division—a group of people or teams in a certain category for a competition

doubles—in tennis, a team of two people playing against another team of two people

Grand Slam—the top four tennis tournaments; the Grand Slam is made up of the Australian Open, the French Open, the U.S. Open, and Wimbledon

junior—a group for players who are younger or have less experience than professionals

pro—short for professional; a person paid for an activity or sport

rank—one's place within a group

record—the number of wins and losses

singles—in tennis, one person playing against one other person

tour—a series of sporting events

tournament—a series of games between several players, ending in one winner

Read More

Diemer, Lauren. *Venus and Serena Williams.* Remarkable People. New York: Av2 by Weigl, 2014.

Gange, Tammy. *Day by Day with Serena Williams.* Randy's Corner: Day by Day With… Hockessin, Del.: Mitchell Lane Publishers, 2016.

Peters, Gregory N. *Serena and Venus Williams Tennis Stars.* North Mankato, Minn.: Capstone Press, 2014.

Internet Sites

FactHound offers a safe, fun way to find Internet sites related to this book. All of the sites on FactHound have been researched by our staff.

Here's all you do:
Visit *www.facthound.com*
Type in this code: 9781491479735

Check out projects, games and lots more at
www.capstonekids.com

Critical Thinking Using the Common Core

1. Serena's father began teaching her tennis at a young age, and she practiced every day. How might this have helped her become a good tennis player? (Integration of Knowledge and Ideas)

2. Reread the text on page 10 and then look at the picture on page 11. What is Serena kissing? (Craft and Structure)

Index